The Dying Breed

Coal Mining History and Memories from North West Durham

by

Hylton Marrs

Edited by

Iain Watson

COUNTY DURHAM BOOKS

Acknowledgements: County Durham Books thank Colin McCulloch for his help with the proof-reading of this book.

Published by County Durham Books, 1993

ISBN 1 897585 03 9

COUNTY DURHAM BOOKS

CONTENTS

1 The North West Durham Coalfield

Together with the coalfield of South Northumberland, of which Durham is a southern extension, the field became known as the "Great Northern Coalfield" and was one of the earliest to be exploited commercially.

Beginning in the first Elizabethan age, coal from this field dominated the London market until the railway age. Sales reached their peak in 1913 (the year of maximum production).

Seams of coal of varying thickness are layered with seat-earth, sand-stone, siltstone and shales in a series of sedimentary cycles, having been deposited during the Carboniferous Age, some 200 million years ago. These coal measures - there were three, upper, middle and lower - were laid down in low lying coastal swamps, estuaries, shallow lagoons and lakes which covered the region successively during that period.

After the deposition of these coal measures, the area was uplifted, the seams dipping from west to east, and then gently folded. Erosion also took place, removing an unknown depth of the upper measure. Only a trace remains, as well as the middle and lower measures, which are the productive seams of the Durham Coalfield.

Durham coals have a wide range of properties, from the soft bright coking coals of the west of the County, to the hard dull coals found mainly in the east. In the upper seams occurred the industrial and house coals, which were among the first to be developed and worked commercially, forming the basis of the London coal trade.

Coal in County Durham can be traced back to Roman times. In 1977 excavation work at Binchester uncovered a 'Pile of coal' dated around the second century. There is evidence that the Romans used coal, as large quantities of it have been found where their forts and settlements were situated. On the Roman sites at Ebchester and Lanchester, coal and cinders were found in what used to be the baths, and also in the smithy.

The next relevant discovery was of a wooden shovel and a leather sandal, which were unearthed by an opencast mining company near Finchale Abbey. They are believed to have been used and worn around the thirteenth century, and are now on exhibition at Beamish Museum.

In medieval times, apart from the drift mine at Collierley (Dipton), which

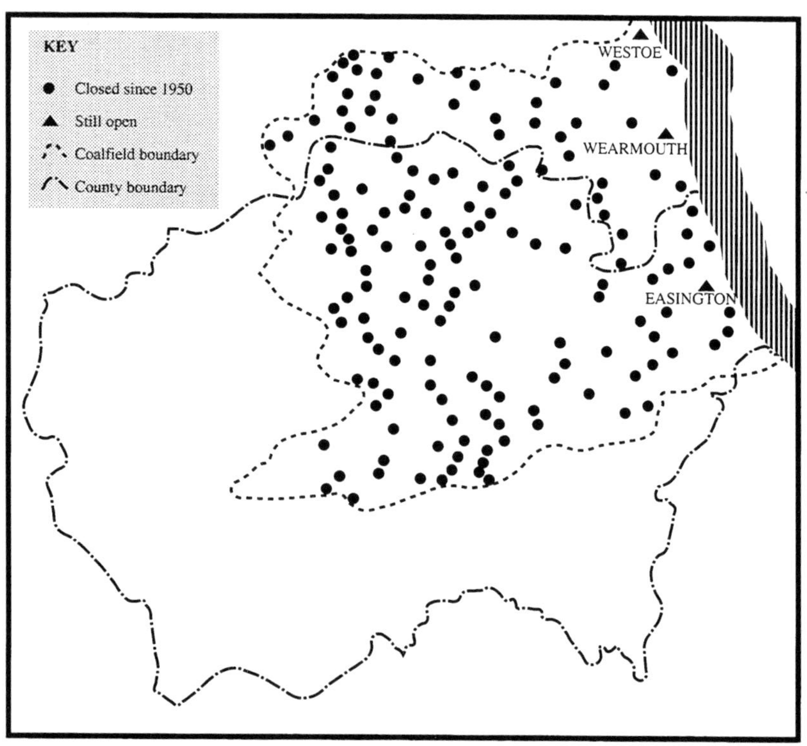

This map of the Durham Coalfield Shows the pits still working in late 1992. The contrast with the number of pits working in 1950 is striking.

was worked in 1333, and workings later at Chopwell in 1586, there were no other mines in the north west of Durham. The nearest mine was at Chester-le-Street, dated 1307, with about twenty more situated to the south and the east, whilst in the north of the region, mines were worked at Ryton, Gateshead, Winlaton and numerous other places.

By the middle of the seventeenth century mines and villages were springing up in nearly all parts of County Durham, although north west Durham was still virtually unmined. The only mining in the area took place at Knitsley about two miles to the south of Consett, and Lanchester four miles to the south-east. The medieval mining interests at Collierley had ended by this time, but mining continued in the Chopwell area.

The seventeenth and eighteenth centuries saw many ore mines throughout the county. Drift mines were being developed and they worked mainly the shallow seams, and the deep or shaft mines were also becoming more popular. In the City of Durham in 1714 coal seams were discovered only

200 yards from the cathedral, but the excessive water problem made it impossible to mine. It was not until 1772 with the introduction of the pumping engine, that this mine and many more like it could be worked.

In the first part of the nineteenth century, the Durham coalfield was spreading in a more north westerly direction from the older areas in the east and south of the County. Coal was being mined as far north as Gateshead, and Consett in the west, with literally scores of mines working in between. There were about forty mines around the Consett and Stanley area, from Delves Lane in the south, to Burnopfield in the north, and Tanfield and Oxhill to the east. The small hamlet of Ebchester doubled its population due to the mines creating a labour market.

With so much coal now available in the area, Derwent Iron Company (later Consett Iron Company) was founded in 1840. It expanded its mining interests, owning and working ten collieries in the area to provide fuel for the blast furnaces.

With so much work available in the area, from the iron works, coal mines and the newly built railways, the small hamlets and villages grew with the influx of workers and their families from many parts of the British Isles, notably Cornwall and Ireland. The latter part of the 1800s was a prosperous time for the mineowners, and this was demonstrated by the type of housing provided for the workers.

The people themselves helped to finance the places of worship such as chapels and churches. Their landlords funded public buildings, institutions, reading rooms, and, to some extent, schools.

The years between 1920—1950 show a drop in the number of mines being worked. The south west of the county was in full production, whilst mines in the other areas were being closed or worked out. Only a handful in the Consett area were still in existence, notably collieries at Delves Lane, Iveston, East Castle and Collierley (Dipton). The Stanley mines fared no better, with only Beamish and Shield Row (with two mines) remaining.

The year 1947 brought about the most significant event in the history of coal mining. The Labour Government nationalised the mines, taking full control and paying compensation to the mineowners. The scene changed dramatically in Durham. The once prolific production in the south west was slowing down, and the east and north east areas were being more extensively mined. In the years between 1950 and 1970, the closure programme of the National Coal Board (N.C.B.) was beginning to take its toll, with mines not thought to be profitable being cleared and the miners being redeployed. After these closures, privately owned drift mines began to appear, licensed by the National Coal Board.

Morrison Busty Pit, Annfield Plain *(Mr Cozens, Sacriston)*

From 1971 to 1992 the face of coal mining has changed once again. The mines around Crook and the Aucklands (Bishop and West), are now privately owned. The only deep mines remaining in County Durham are Vane Tempest/Seaham and Easington. In late 1992 both of these are threatened as part of a major pit closure programme. The end of coalmining in Durham, unthinkable only a few years ago, may now be in sight.

The largest settlement in north west Durham is Consett. Growing from a small village in 1840, it owes its situation and consequent expansion to the discovery of iron ore and coal in the vicinity. The establishment of the Iron Works and its products made the name of Consett famous around the world. Its need for good coking coal and the development of coal mining made Consett Iron Company one of the largest coal owners in the north of England. Many villages grew up in the area to house the thousands of workers required to operate the Iron Works and many of the collieries. At this period of time (1992) there is no sign of the mighty site of Consett Iron Company. Landscaped and grassed over it has been returned to nature. The many villages near to Consett have become dormitories for workers to travel to Durham and Newcastle, whilst Consett's role as a major production unit is over.

The first whinstone workings at Consett date from 1837, and were followed by the creation of the Derwent Iron Company in 1840. The company was first founded to exploit local iron ore deposits which were mined along with coal at three of the four Consett collieries at this time. The collapse of the Northumberland and District Bank which backed the Derwent Iron Company in 1857, brought a crisis to the area. This was finally resolved in 1864 with the creation of the Consett Iron Company.

As the Industrial Revolution got under way, and new techniques and processes became commonplace, the demand for coke became critical. Coke was first used by Abraham Darby in 1709 to fuel his iron furnace at Coalbrookdale in Shropshire. In 1735, the first blast furnaces using coke as a fuel in the north east of England were situated at Whitehill, near Chester-le-Street. It was not until the opening out of the Durham Coalfield in the Consett area, with its excellent coking coal seams, that coke making was developed at Consett, in the mid-nineteenth century.

In the National Coal Board office (now British Coal) at Gateshead, reference is made to the Blackhill Busty seam plane, this was dated 1849. The plan shows an 'outcrop' of coal midway between Medomsley Road and Consett, and the siting of the collieries along the escarpment was perhaps instrumental in the foundation of the Consett Iron Works on the site it once occupied. The mines on the escarpment at Consett were known as the number 1, 2, 3 and 4 collieries. These were dual purpose mines, excavating coal and ironstone. Mining these two minerals in one mine was no doubt a great attraction for investment at this time.The No.1 colliery was situated less than one hundred yards from the present roundabout at the northern end of Medomsley Road.

No. 1 mine was a coal and ironstone mine, with the minerals running in seams very close to each other. The coal seam was the Harvey, or Townley, at three feet thick. Ironstone was worked from the Tenbrand seam, seven feet thick.

No. 2 mine was only a short distance away on the edge of what is now the Belle View football ground. This was a coal mine only.

No. 3 mine was about 300 yards due south and towards Consett, near what is now Sherburn Park. Coal and ironstone were mined.

No.4 mine was situated near what is now Hartington Street, and mined the same coal and ironstone seams as Nos.1 and 3 pits.

The sites of these early collieries are shown on the accompanying map of the present Consett area. There is no visible trace of the shafts, although they are documented in the first edition of the Ordnance Survey of 1856. Research shows that these four collieries were closed before 1849.

The plan of the "Busty" seam which was worked in the Berryedge and Crookhall royalties, which were dated 1849, shows a shaft mine which is named as the Consett Coal Pit.

CONSETT, a small town in the township of CONSIDE-CUM-KNITSLEY and parochial chapelry of Medomsley and formed into an ecclesiastical parish in 1862, from the parishes of Ebchester and Lanchester; it is 12 miles north-west from Durham and 14 south-west from Newcastle, in the North Western division of the county, west division of Chester ward, Lanchester union, head of the petty sessional division of Consett, Consett county court district, rural deanery of Ryton and archdeaconry and diocese of Durham. Consett and Blackhill station, quarter of a mile north, and Knitsley station, 1½ miles south-west, are on the Consett branch of the North Eastern railway. Consett adopted the Local Government Act, 1858, in 1865, and is governed by a Local Board of 12 members. Christ Church, erected in 1866, is a noble edifice of stone, in the Norman style, consisting of chancel, nave of four bays, north aisle and a western tower, with pinnacles, containing 6 bells: there are sittings for about 700 persons. The register dates from the year 1866. The living is a vicarage, yearly value £300, with residence in the gift of the Crown and the Bishop of Durham alternately, and held since 1864 by the Rev. Frederick Steggall There are Wesleyan, Baptist and Primitive Methodis chapels and Salvation Army barracks. There are collierie in this township. The Consett ironworks, established in 1841, situated in this township, are very extensive; some idea may be formed of the extent by the following statistics:—about 6,000 hands of all sorts are employed, about 3,000 in coal mining and 3,000 in the manufacture of coke, pig iron, steel and iron plates &c.: about 1,000,000 tons of coal are raised, and 500,000 tons of coke are made yearly: there are 7 large blast furnaces capable of turning out 700 tons each of pig iron per week: the company are engaged in mining in the north of Spain, whence they procure their hematite ore: about 2,300 tons of stee plates are made per week, and 500 tons of iron plates the bulk of which is consumed in ship building, boiler making and bridge building. The New Town Hall, situated at the corner of Front street and Middle street, is a large stone building, erected in 1884, from the designs of Mr. W. Lister Newcombe, of Newcastle-on-Tyne, at a cost of £5,000: the ground floor is occupied by shops, offices and the reading room, library and billiard room of the Consett Recreation Society; above is a large hall, which will hold 1,000 persons. The Theatre Royal is situated in Trafalgar street, and will hold 700 persons. The Infirmary, a building of stone, erected in 1876, is supported by the Consett Iron Co. and none but employés of the company are admitted; it will hold 50 patients. Consett Hall is the residence of William Jenkins esq. J.P. The Ecclesiastical Commissioners are the lords of the manor. The Earl of Coventry, the Consett Iron Co. Limited and William Robert Taylor esq. are chief landowners. The soil is clay. The chief crops are potatoes, barley, oats and pasture. The area of the township is 3,119 acres; rateable value, £31,150: the population in 1881 was, of the township 6,746, and of the parish 7,708.

Sexton, George Jackson.

Kelly's Directory, 1891

There were other collieries in the near vicinity, notably Delves Lane Pit (then called the Latterday Saints Pit because of the owners' religion). The colliery had a shaft which was sunk to the Busty Seam, a depth of 130 feet. The pit at this time employed 123 people and supplied 26 coke ovens.

Tin Mill Colliery or Mount Pleasant Pit was situated at the top of what is now Consett Park, about 100 yards from Derwentside College. The seams worked were the Busty and 3/4 seam. By 1898 the pit was exhausted, although its name lives on in the shape of a nearby pub "The Mount Pleasant".

There were many more shafts sunk at various times around the end of the nineteenth century. The successful ones are remembered and recorded, while others were exploited, abandoned and forgotten as soon as their commercial value waned.

The entry for Consett in 'Kelly's County Directory of Northumberland and Durham' dated 1891 shows Consett developing into a sizeable town. Already Consett could boast many buildings and organisations. In 1865 the town adopted the Local Government Act (1858) and Consett was governed by a board, or committee, of twelve members. Other notable achievements included the Church of England, Christ Church, and St. Patrick's (for the Catholic community). Chapels included Wesleyan, Baptist and Primitive Methodist.

There was also a Salvation Army barracks which housed the first brass band under the Salvation Army banner in the world. The infirmary erected in 1876 was fully supported by Consett Iron Company, and nobody but their employees could be treated there. The Town Hall was built in 1884 at a cost of £5000. Schools built in this period include:

1. The British School built in 1840.

2 . St. Patrick' s School built in 1868.

3. The National School built in 1875.

4. The Wesleyan School built in 1879.

Newspapers at this time were The Consett Guardian and the Consett

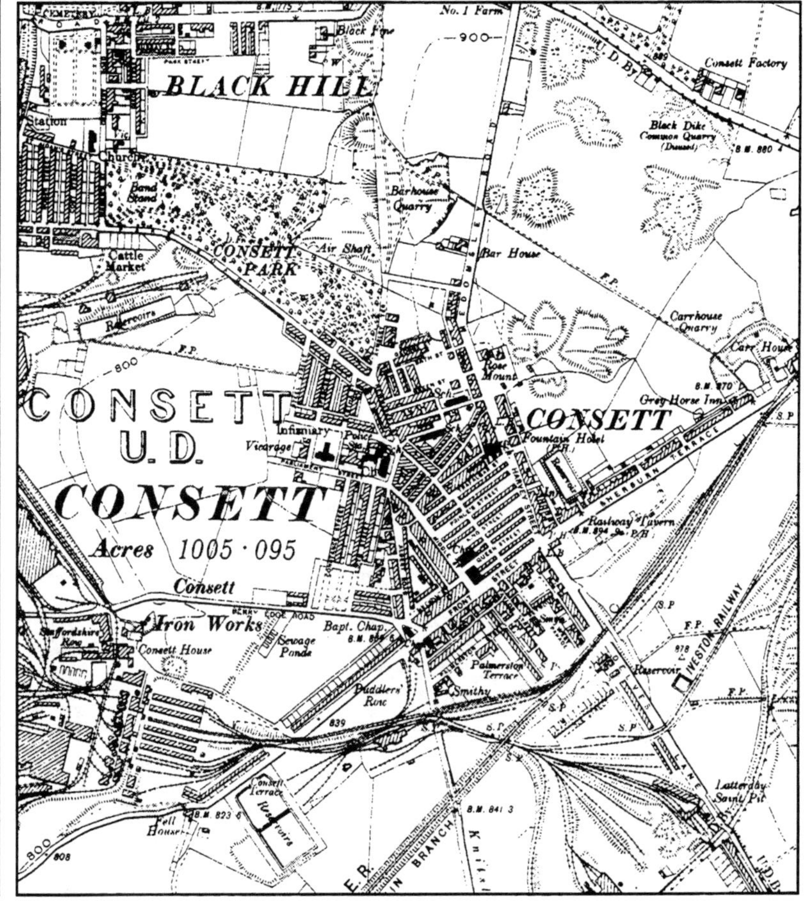

Consett, 1899

Morrison North and South Pits, Annfield Plain *(Mr Cozens, Sacriston)*

Chronicle. Law and Order was served by holding the Petty Sessions, which were held in the Police Station (built in 1877 at a cost of £4000).

In the fifty years from the 1840s to 1890s, Consett had grown from a village into a town of great importance. Consett Iron Company was by far the biggest employer. 3000 worked at the iron works and 3000 at the coal mines owned by them in the area – a vast increase since 1857.

The extent of the coal deposits in the area was without a doubt the main reason for the success of the area. Consett Iron Company became bigger and stronger and it monopolised the coal industry in the area.

Following are the names of the major collieries which were owned by the Consett Iron Company and the date on which the shaft was sunk. Between

Population of Consett, from Census returns

Year	Population
1801	**139**
1811	**141**
1821	**146**
1831	**195**
1841	**2777**

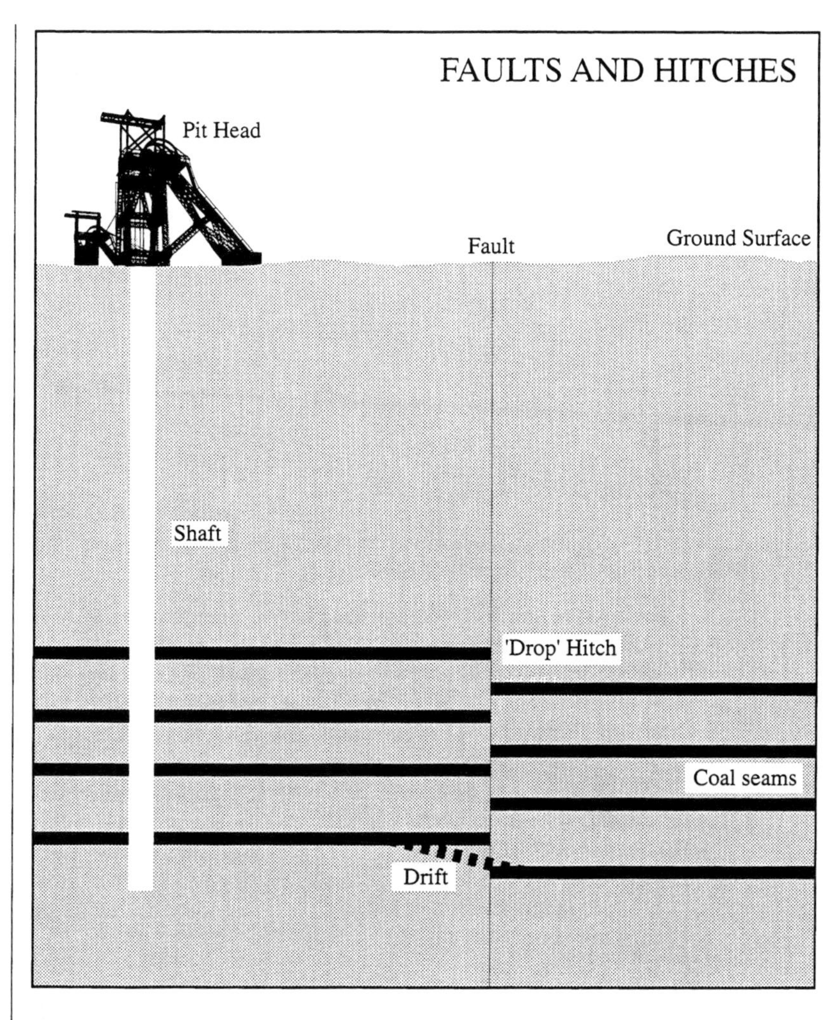

1800 and 1947, Consett Iron Company owned thirteen collieries and dozens of drift mines which are forgotten and unrecorded.

1. Garesfield Bute	Sunk 1800
2. Medomsley Busty	Sunk 1839
3. Blackhill Colliery	Sunk 1840
4. Marley Hill	Sunk 1844
5. Delves Lane	Sunk 1847

6. Eden (Leadgate)	Sunk 1850
7. Iveston	Sunk 1850
8. Delight (Dipton)	Sunk 1854
9. Iceston	Sunk 1854
10. Derwent (Medomsley)	Sunk 1856
11. Westwood	Sunk 1871
12. Chopwell (No 1)	Sunk 1896
13. Chopwell (No 2)	Sunk 1906

Chopwell

No account of coal mining in north west Durham would be complete without a mention of the village of Chopwell.

Situated to the north of Consett district, the mines were owned by the Consett Iron Company. In 1891 boring proved the coal Reserves and the Iron Company sank two shafts in the north of the village. However, the strata had been disturbed by a number of major geological faults, which affected mining operations in the area. The 'Ninety Fathom Dyke' runs west-south-west to east-north-east, across the north of the village, causing the coal seams to disappear. If the seam reappears below the normal level it is called a 'Drop Hitch '. If the seam appears above the normal level it is called a 'Rise Hitch'. The distance above or below could be many fathoms (a fathom is 6 feet or 1.82 metres). Drilling took place in an attempt to find the coal again and when found a drift had to be driven up or down as the case may be.

This was a very expensive operation as the drift was driven in solid stone, so there was no coal to finance the operation. Running south-east to north-west across the middle of the coal reserves was the 'Tantobie Fault', a drop hitch of 100 feet. This was also financially impossible to pass through. This left most of Chopwell sitting on an Island of Coal', unapproachable from any other mining operation. This proved very lucrative for the owners over the years. The most productive year was 1913, when 250,000 tons of coal were mined and transported out of the village of Chopwell.

Consett and District in 1992

As one travels around Consett and district in 1992 it is very hard to understand the traumatic changes which have taken place over the past two hundred years. The mining industry which existed from 1840 to 1980 cannot be traced. Pit heaps have been levelled and planted with trees, and all signs of the pit buildings and pit shafts have long since disappeared, while the branch lines connecting the collieries have been lifted.

The Iron and Steel Industry ceased to exist in 1980 and all signs of the mighty Consett Iron Company, have gone, sites re-grassed, buildings non-existent and the huge working areas returned to nature. The people instead of flocking in their thousands to their place of work on the infamous three shifts pattern 6 to 2, 2 to 10, and 10 to 6 have retired and the younger working generation has to make do with working "day shift" in a small factory on one of the many trading Estates which sprang up to try and utilise the huge pool of labour which was available.

The main line railways which served the Consett area from 1850 to 1980 are now country walks, and when one uses them and looks towards Consett it is difficult to realise the change in the local environment, and what it would have looked like 100 years previous, with collieries dotted around the district, and the furnaces and slag heaps of Consett Iron Company lighting up the sky.

Many people will say the changes are for the better. The work was hard and conditions dangerous in any of the jobs that were available, but in someways people were happier then with full time employment, and had a bob or two in their pockets.

2 Pit Men and their Lives

The pits and the pitmen had their own way of life - which is now disappearing fast. The pitmen had their own dialect - pitmatic - and there was also a whole range of technical terms unique to the mining industry (see glossary). Working practices in the mines were also different to those in other industries and there is a particular history, before Nationalisation in 1947, of confrontation between pitmen and coal owners. This section of the book records some details of the superstitions and of the working practices in the pits which are now almost forgotten.

Superstitions in the Mines

With the work underground being so dangerous and akin to slavery it was no wonder that superstitions abounded among the miners.

When the pit pony was introduced into the mines it was only natural that it would be incorporated into the web of mining superstitions. Many miners used the ponies as a kind of forecast for the events of the day. If the pony was fit and in good spirits then the day would go well, but if the pony was ill and restless, then there was trouble ahead for the men who

Pelton Fell miners waiting to go down in the cage. *(Pelton Fell Action Group)*

worked with this particular animal. This was taken so seriously that men would actually refuse to work if the pony was ill, convinced that if they did so they would be caught in a rock fall or injured in any one of the many ways in which a man could be hurt down the pit. The ponies were not the only ones stranded in the web of superstition that hemmed in the life of the miner. Some men would always follow an exact routine when going to work, at least half convinced that any deviation would bring catastrophe.

To meet a woman on his way to work on the night shift would result in the miner returning home, and he would be reluctant to go to work if he forgot anything and had to re-enter the house.

Birds and animals were also included in this folklore.The sighting of a crow perched on the pulley wheels would result in the miner refusing to descend the shaft. Likewise a crowing cockerel was regarded as very bad luck, and any ornament or picture of birds was always arranged to face the door in order that the bad luck they were thought to bring would fly out of the house. The white rabbit was also considered to be unlucky, and to see one on the way to work meant a swift about turn.

On cavilling day the miner's wife would put a cat into the unheated oven, if it came out alive then her man would draw a good cavil. Another superstition about cats was that one was never allowed to die in the house.

Miners were very concerned about their strength and a number of superstitions were related to this, if a miner washed his back then he thought it would weaken him. If a man had any aches or pains then a length of wool tied around the affected part was supposed to help.

The festive seasons of Christmas and New Year had their own superstitions, many of which are still adhered to. Mince pies were lucky and a happy month in the coming year was guaranteed for every different pie you ate. On New Year's Eve the front door step would be whitened. Money was placed in the pockets of all the children to ensure a prosperous year. The pantry was thoroughly cleansed and bread was freshly baked. Woe betide the family if a hole or 'coffin' was found inside one of their loaves.

First Footing is still an important part of the New Year festivities. The first foot had to be dark haired and a bachelor - and never a woman. The first foot always carried a gift which consisted of something for the fire, plus salt and bread. The first foot must not leave without partaking of food and drink. The next day nothing must be taken from the house in case the good luck would be taken with it.

Family occasions had their own superstitions. A new born baby must be given gifts, especially by neighbours. The infant was taken to three neighbours' homes and was given the three necessities: salt, bread and tea.

If a baby cried at its baptism it was a good omen as the devil had left the child. Before leaving for the church a parcel of the christening cake was wrapped up and given to the first person of the opposite sex to the child seen on the way to church.

Three young miners ready for the pit. *(Arts, Libraries and Museums Department, Durham County Council)*

Marriage also had a set of superstitions, some still in vogue. It was supposed to be unlucky to marry in May or in Lent: 'If you marry in lent you'll live to repent'. The colour green must never be worn by the bride and she should always wear 'something old, something new, something borrowed, something blue'. On leaving the bride's home it was customary to throw pennies to those watching. This was known as a 'hoy oot'.

Death also had its own rites and superstitions. To hear bells during the night time was regarded as a sign of death. If a picture fell from a wall, dogs were heard howling or three crows seen sitting in a row it was thought that a fatality was imminent. Visitors coming to see the deceased were expected to touch the corpse as by doing so they showed that they bore no ill feeling towards the departed person. The door of the room in which the body lay was left open to allow evil spirits to leave. Mirrors in the room were covered so that they could not reflect the deceased and trap his or her spirit. The blinds in the house, and those of neighbours, were closed until after the funeral

Bidders, two in number, were sent to inform friends and neighbours about the arrangements for the funeral. These bidders were always men. Wearing top hats they went to the houses to invite the occupants to the funeral and the tea following that. On the day of the funeral the coffin was placed outside and the mourners stood around singing hymns before the procession to church or chapel. Mourners who had been bidden walked in front of the coffin. Six young people wearing black crepe sashes crossed over their chests carried wreaths. Other mourners walked behind. After the funeral the mourners and those bidden returned to the house for the traditional funeral tea of boiled ham, tongue, pease pudding and pickles.

The death of a miner killed in the pit brought the whole village to the funeral and the colliery band played the Dead March. On the first pay day after the death a colleague of the deceased would stand near the pay office to collect from those being paid. Money collected was given to the dead miner's immediate family.

Following the funeral it was traditional for friends and family to attend church the Sunday following and also on the 'year's mind', the anniversary of the death.

Cavilling Day

From the early days of mining the method of coal production in the Durham mines was 'Bord and Pillar'. This method was the only one in existence. Depending on where you were mining the name changed to 'Bord and Wall' or 'Bord and Stall', but the method was the same.

The seam of coal being worked (for example, Busty or Brockwell) and the direction it was being worked in (for example, north or south) gave the name of the district (for example, Busty South District).

The miner's workplace was called the cavil and your cavil or place to hew was distributed on the first Saturday of the quarter. This was called Cavilling Saturday.

The miners' representives would present themselves at the colliery office on this day along with the management. The number of work places (cavils) would be given a number eg 1 to 50 . The coal hewers for that district were also given numbers. These were then placed in containers and drawn out alternately, that is a cavil then a hewer's name. At the end of the lottery each coal hewer had a place of work for the next three months.

If you were lucky you would draw a cavil which had a good roof, was dry, and the coal reasonably soft so you could make a moderate living for the next three months. If you were unlucky the roof could be dangerous, with wet conditions and hard coal. You were stuck with your choice for three months until the next cavilling day. You could not exchange cavils during this time, so your standard of living could suffer. The boys putting had the same system. Many a prayer was said, and many a candle lighted, when the cavilling day drew near, because miners in their own way were a superstitious breed.

Coal Owner's Methods of Extortion

Management at the time used various methods of extracting money from the miners. If the mine had just opened the piece work rates had to be set, these would be determined for each working coal seam according to the coal thickness and hardness and condition in general.

The management would employ a 'crack hewer' or 'score fixer' on a private contract. This man was far superior to the usual coal hewer, and was able to hew and fill many more tubs than the average hewer. The management would argue that if this man could do it, then the average hewer could. So the score price would be fixed on this man's production. Consequently the hewers would try and increase their production to match that of the 'crack hewer' at a low score price. When the prices had been fixed to the management's liking, this man would be paid off and he would move on to another embryo mine to repeat the action.

Another management ploy was to introduce the '21 score', that meant that the coal hewer had to mine 21 tubs of coal and only get paid for a score (20). So the management was getting 8—10 cwts of coal free for every 20 tubs mined and paid for. The miners were ordered to press down the coal which was loaded into the tub to enable them to get an extra amount loaded. This meant that the coal hewer got paid per tub of 8—10 cwts filled and the owner got the extra free.

The most detested system was the 'lay outs'. This enabled the owner to fine the hewer reponsible for filling the tub and confiscate the value of its contents from his wages. Management ruled that if a certain weight of stone was found in the tub mixed with the coal, then the man reponsible was cheating. The offending stone would be put into a basket and put on display along with the man's name and token number to show the rest of the workforce it did not pay to try and cheat the owner.

The miners attempted to get justice by employing their own man paid by them to check the 'Master Weighman'. He was usually a union official and his title was 'Check Weighman'.

3 The Life and Times of a Durham Pit Village - Annfield Plain

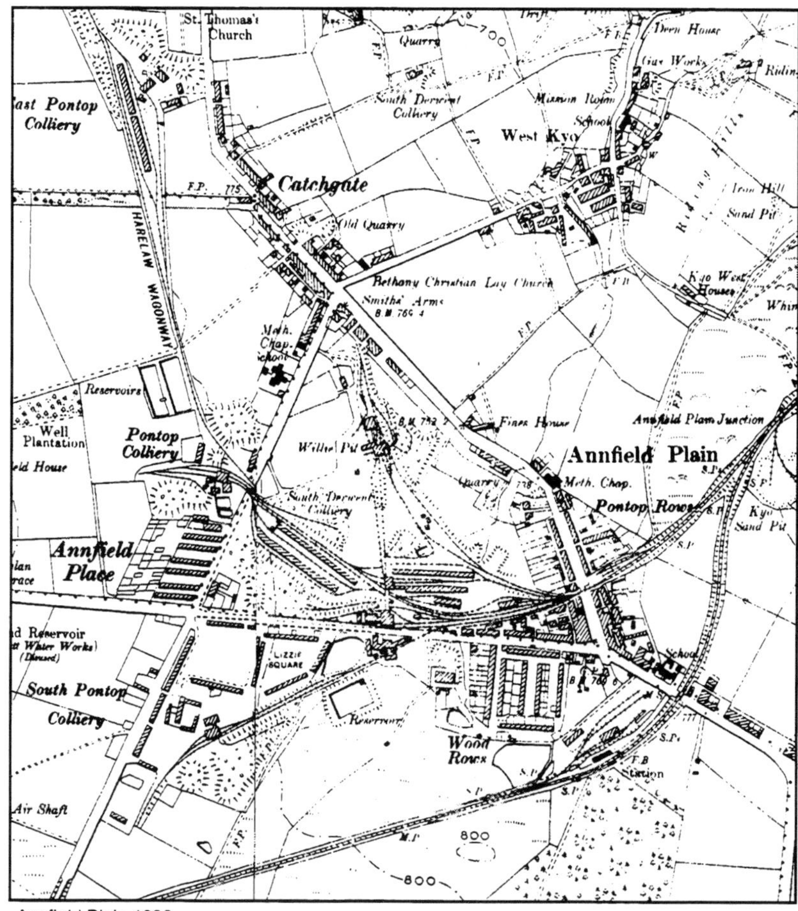

Annfield Plain 1898

Annfield Plain is situated five miles to the east of the township of Consett. The village owes its name to the fact of its importance to the Stanhope and Tyne Railway. A standing engine was situated on the Loud Hill, near Annfield House, to pull wagons up the steep eastern slope of Pontop Pike. This became known as the Annfield Plane or slope.

Coal mining did not flourish until the 1880s when numerous shafts were sunk and mines opened up in the area. The various sites of these pits became communities within a community - places like the 'Lizzie' at Greencroft.

Coal mining in the Annfield Plain area began a gradual decline in the 1930s. The Morrison Busty colliery was the last pit to be sunk in the district in 1925. It had a very short life as collieries go and closed in 1973, ending the era of coal mining at Annfield Plain. The names of former pits are still remembered, such as the Busty, the North Pit, the Willie, the Lizzie, the Charlie and dozens of others. The names and the memories remain.

South Pontop Colliery (Lizzie Pit)

After 66 years existence as a going concern, this colliery near Annfield Plain and familiarly called the 'Lizzie Pit' closed in 1928. It was dismantled with the coal practically exhausted, owing to high cost of production, increased rates, and low selling prices. Messrs. Ritson, the owners, were reluctantly compelled to cease operations as the only coal left available for working, which might have provided a few more months of employment, consisted of thin ribs and stooks left in the goaves of former years. This would have entailed considerable expense in searching for and working.

During the whole of this period the colliery had been owned by the Ritson family. A grant was given to Henry Ritson of Shotley Bridge (Timber Merchant) to win and work the Hutton Seam and overlying seams over an area of approximately 162 acres for a term of ten years from 1st November 1860.

Thirty acres of land was acquired from the Clavering Estate who were the surface owners. Sinking operations were commenced on ground covered with ling and coarse grass a short distance from the road crossing at the foot of the Loud Hill and towards Greencroft. As capital was limited only one shaft was at first sunk, this was known as the Old Pit or Lizzie Pit. The first sod was cut in August 1861, and good progress was made with the sinking. The Five Quarter and Brass Thill Seams were reached at a depth of 171 feet and the first coals were drawn on 9th December 1861.

The Shield Row Seam at a depth of 51 feet, with a section of 3 feet 6 inches Top Coal, 1 foot of band and 1 foot of bottom coal was passed as not being suitable for working at that particular time. The Five Quarter Seam with a section of 5 foot 6 inches and the Brass Thill Seam with a section of 5 foot 6 inches were practically together, only separated by a shale band 12 inches thick.

A commencement was immediately made to win and get out coal in the

Five Quarter and for the 15 days worked in December 1861, there were 1,842 tons of coal raised. Mr. Thomas Simpson from Medomsley Colliery was the first resident viewer or overman appointed. He was not long in developing and opening out the pit. In the following year 64,041 tons were brought to bank from the Five Quarter and Brass Thill Seams. For the 245 days worked there was an average of 261 tons per day. In 1866 the output from this shaft winding with two single tub cages was 155,260 tons for 288 days worked or 540 tons per day. This was the record output year for the colliery.

In the latter part of 1866 a commencment was made to sink what is known as the new pit or Willie Pit a few yards to the east of the Lizzie Shaft, for the purpose of working the Hutton Seam which was reached on 21st October 1867 at a depth of 341 feet. There was a section of 3 foot 6 inches Top Coal, Band 1 foot 6 inches, Bottom Coal 4 foot 6 inches, all of splendid quality. Under the above coal and separated from it by a band varying in thickness from 2 to 5 feet was the Little Hutton or Section Seam, 22 inches to 24 inches thick which had in recent years been worked as a separate seam from under the overlying goaf of the Hutton Seam. Sinking was completed and this shaft was fitted with wire rope guides for conductors which were rather an innovation at that time. They proved very satisfactory during the whole period worked. Two of the original guides were still being used when the last coal was being drawn at this shaft.

Opening was rapidly proceeded with so that within six months an output of 160 tons per day was being raised from this seam. A connection between the two shafts was made at the Five Quarter Seam making an additional output for it. Previous to this there had only been the one outlet to the Lizzie Shaft. To ventilate the Hutton Seam and to afford a second outlet a small staple 3 foot in diameter was sunk down to the Main Coal Seam into Messrs Bowes and Partners Pontop working. This served until it was decided to deepen the Old Pit or Lizzie Pit in 1872.

Workings in the Shield Row started in December 1877 and, in August 1892, the Little Hutton or Section Seam was opened out. Output fluctuated considerably, getting as low as 110 tons per day in 1918, with an average of 327 tons per day during the whole working period. Additional areas to work were made by an exchange with East Pontop Colliery in 1883. A sub-lease area in Shield Row Seam and Hutton Section Seam was obtained from the South Derwent Coal Company in 1899, prolonging the life of the colliery considerably. A total of 5,543,790 tons was raised at the colliery. This is approximately 95% of the theoretical quantity that the same should produce over the area worked.

In addition a very large quantity of stone was drawn which was visible in the high heap at the colliery and estimated to contain at least 250,000 tons. Much of this came from the working of the Little Hutton Seam and from goaf ridding to recover the stooks left in the Five Quarter and Brass Thill Seams. Owing to their thickness and proximity it was a difficult matter to work wholly out in the first workings, thus necessitating the going over of the area a second time and in some cases a third time. No gas was ever found and nothing but open lights were used. The quantity of water dealt with was not large, with the exception of the Shield Row Seam in which a steam pump operated in the years 1883 to 1886 to cope with leakage from the Consett Water Compan's reservoir on the Loud Hill. This leakage became so excessive that it was abandoned as a reservoir, the water level went back to normal and the pump was taken out. What remained was dealt with by bore holes and holings into adjacent workings where it finally gravitated into the Old Pontop Water Level, having its outlet near Lintz Green. This drains the Pontop district to approximately 70 fathoms level to deal with a fault in the Hutton Seam and a small electric generating plant was installed in 1891, and an electric pump put in. This was the first to be used in the Annfield Plain area and one of the earliest in the Durham Coalfield.

On the whole the colliery was remarkably free from serious accidents, the fatalities numbering eleven, all occurring singly. These were:

D. Dawson a putter in the Brass Thill killed by a fall of stone in 1863

John Errington died in the Pit from apoplexy on 14th June 1848

George Barker died in the pit from apoplexy in October 1870

M.Berrigan, coal hewer, died from injuries received from a fall of band in the Hutton Seam in 1875

William Cobbledick, stoneman, killed by a fall of stone in the Shield Row Seam in November 1891

John Tucker, pony driver, fell out of the cage in the Willie Pit Shaft in 1894

John William Robson, coal hewer, killed by a fall of coal and stone in the Brass Thill Seam on 16th November 1897

John Armstrong, coal hewer, crushed between the pack wall and a tub in the Section Seam on 29th May 1894

Rising Platten, deputy, died from blood poisoning on 12th February 1901 due to a cut on the head from an old rail

James Beckam, shifter, crushed between tub and pack wall in the Section Seam on 23rd October 1902

Charles Alderson, stone putter, died when his head was crushed between timber and tub in the Section Seam on 19th March 1909

John W. Cross, electric hauler attendant, caught by a rope and drawn onto the drum of the hauler in the Hutton Seam on 4th April 1919,

For the housing of the workmen, 90 wooden houses were built in 1861 to 1862 adjoining the Annfield Plain to Consett Road. Stone houses were also built facing the Greencroft Road, with a short row of wood single room houses at right angles next to the Greencroft end. In addition, the Manager's house and two overmen's houses were erected in the colliery yard. The whole made a very open and pleasant lay-out. Owing to serious damage by subsidence the whole of the above with the exception of the three in the colliery yard were demolished in the years 1905 to 1909.

Messrs. Ritson purchased the freehold of the land in 1904, and the houses were replaced by those now standing - 13 brick built houses in West View Terrace, 37 stone-built in Derwent Terrace and another 20 houses in Pontop Terrace. Sites for Fair View Terrace were sold to individual purchasers who built their own. This also applied to the houses beyond West View Terrace.

Previous to the extension of the Consett Water Company's mains over the Loud Hill, the domestic water supply for the inhabitants was obtained from a standage in the Shield Row Seam. It was pumped from a beam pumping set worked off the old pit winding engine and delivered to a wooden storage tank adjoining the colliery shops, from which it was rationed out daily at stated times. It was not unusual for the pump to be out of action and when this occurred, tin cans, wooden skeels and other receptacles were sent down the pit in the cage, filled and sent up again after coal drawing had finished for the day. On such occasions the pit heap presented a very busy appearance with women and children seeking their water supply. It was therefore a great boon when the Consett water supply was made available.

Mr. H. Ritson was not unmindful of the education of the children. In 1863 he brought Mr. Edwards Gray and Mrs. Gray as schoolmaster and mistress, providing them with a house and placing at their disposal for school accommodation a large detached wooden building standing at the north west corner of the top square of houses at the crossing of the Greencroft and Loud Roads. This building had been previously used as a provision store or 'Tommy Shop'. Here the children were taught reading, writing and a little reckoning. Reading commenced with the A.B.C. cards, followed by the A.B. ab. primer and spelling books, finishing off with the Bible. Writing was taught by straight strokes and gibby sticks or pot hooks then the various letters until they could write their name. Arithmetic by learning the numbers and multiplication tables, then going through simple addition. The girls were instructed in knitting and sewing, instead of so much arithmetic. After the death of Mr. Gray in July 1875 the school in the last few years was simply an infant school. The older children attended the school at Annfield Plain which had now been built. In September 1870, Mr. U.A. Ritson took full control over the Colliery until December 1899 when it was registered as a limited company under the name of U.A.Ritson and Sons Ltd.

The names and period of employment of the various officials in connection:

Checkviewer or Agent

1.	James Gray	1860 — ?
2.	C. Berkley	? — 1899
3.	Col. J.R. Ritson	1899 — 1928

Managers

1	Thomas Simpson	1860 — 1869
2	Stephen Launders	1869 — 1871
3	Henry Greener	1871 — 191
4	J.P. Kirkup	1901 — 1916
5	Jos Snaith	1916 — 1928

Overmen

1	S. Saunders	1862 — 1869
2	W. Eltringham	1869 — 1873

Fore Overman / Under Managers

1	C. Green	1868 — 1898 (Willie Pit)
2	W. Greener	1873 — 1898 (Lizzie Pit)
3	J. Snaith	1899 — 1901
4	R. Summerbell	1901 — 1905

5	J. Snaith	1905 — 1912
6	G. Rogers	1912 — 1920
7	C. Storey	1920 — Closure.

Back Overman

1	W. Eltringham	1906 — 1928

Master Shifters

1	S. Thompson	1860
2	M. Dodds	
3	H. Stephenson	
4	W. Vickers	
5	T. Snaith	
6	R. Graham	
7	J. Snaith	1928

Engineers

1	H. Dodds	1860 — 1899
2	J. Stephenson	1899 — ?
3	J. Smedley	?
4	P. Stokoe	1912 — 1928

Keeker

1	T. Robson	1860 — 1871
2	R. Robson	1871 — 1921
3	E. Bambridge	1921 — 1926
4	W. Bambridge	1926 — 1927

Cashier and Colliery Clerk

1	Thomas Thirlwell	1860
2	Thomas Wilkin	
3	G. Gair	
4	M. Heckels	
5	Thomas Dyson	
6	Miss E. Eddy	1927

During the whole of the period the relationship between the owners and the employees was most satisfactory and apart from County stoppages no loss of work occurred due to disputes with the exception of seven days in 1925.

The colliery from its commencement had the reputation of good working conditions, and there was no difficulty in getting a good class of workmen. Many of those on the last pay sheets were representatives of families whose names appear on the pay sheets of 1862 to 1872, for example, Robson, Harrison, Iceton, Ross, Stobbart, Snaith, Storey, Pinkerton, Coburn Elliott and Weston.

The Old Pit or Lizzie Shaft was filled up completely by Wm and Thos Snaith with material from the adjoining stoneheap. It was completed on 18th June 1928. The New Pit, the Willie Shaft, had been covered over with a covering of railway rails and concrete l5inches thick resting on the shaft walling. Completed on October the 22nd 1927, it was surrounded by a 14 inches thick and 6 foot high brick wall.

The Lizzie, like all colliery villages in the 1860s and 1870s, was isolated and quite different from what we know now. In those days there were no passenger railways, no buses, and hardly any bicycles.

Nichol Bean of Park Head Farm journeyed to Newcastle on pay Saturdays with a long cart taking passengers and carrying back their marketing. The nearest railway station was Lintz Green to which people walked. T. Humphrey of Loud Farm carried on with the journeys and was later succeeded by W. Humphreys of Annfield Plain and P. Hammel of Kyo. Later R. Hodgson, John Humble and James Rostron made the journey twice a week between Annfield Plain and Newcastle, on Wednesdays (Market Day) and Saturdays. The fare was one shilling each way, and sufficed for all the travelling requirements of the people in the immediate neighbourhood. People did not travel very often or very far from home. A day in Newcastle once a year was looked upon as quite an event and preparations in the way of saving for it made weeks before hand.

In summer time brake trips to South Shields and Sunderland were usually run for a day's outing by the seaside. People however enjoyed themselves even in those days and more especially by their own efforts. The Lizzie was in no way backward in this respect for in those years it boasted a cricket club equal to any in north west Durham. Players included the brothers Stobbart, Broadbent, Parrin, Hunter with Bobby Bell and Bob Tindall.

Matches in those days were generally arranged with neighbouring cricket clubs. Usually a supper, an outfit of cricket belts, caps, or in some cases simply a bat or ball was played for. They usually took place on Saturdays and were all day fixtures, commencing early in the afternoon and continuing until the evening with intervals for rolling the rig in the field on which the stumps were pitched.

Considering such disadvantages as having no levelled cricket pitches or turfed ground, good and exciting games were witnessed. A junior team was organized by Mr. Alderson, the Consett Water Company resident agent at the Loud Reservoir who also played very successfully for several seasons. The players often appeared on the field dressed in clown costumes and also gave a good display of cricket. Their mountebank antics and by-play gave great amusement and their services were in great request for sports and field days held in the locality. Players in this included: Tom and Jack Stobbart, Alex Carrol, John Willie Robson, Tom Tindall, Richy Robson, Sam Smith, Tom Snaith, Jimmy Smith and Bob Harrison. In the eighteen eighties football was coming into vogue, cricket declined and the young players went more for football with several joining up and playing for the Red Stars, one of the earliest teams in the district.

Pigeon flying also had a large number of followers, the brothers Robinson, Harry Ashburn, George Green, John W Robson, and G.Applegarth having famous lofts of pigeons with matches and sweeps being frequently flown.

Quoiting, handball playing and dog running (both whippets and greyhounds) had their followers, so there was seldom a pay week-end without some match or other taking place. Harry Stephenson, a well known greyhound trainer, living at the Lizzie in this period was the possessor of a stop-watch and was always in great demand as starter and time-keeper for these events.

In addition to the above sports there was generally an annual visit of a circus company, usually "Swallows" or "Gunnets". The men at the colliery dug out and banked up a proper circus ring in the middle of the high square which made an ideal pitching ground for the circus. Occasionally wild beast shows would arrive and give displays. A regular visitor for many years was Collet and Co, with his wooden booth, which he set up for three or four weeks and provided dramatic entertainment in.

Such entertainments as Maria Martin and the Long Pach were produced and received with great gusto. Another entertainer called Carter travelling with a troop of gymnasts, singers and dancers frequently came. He usually set up at the end of the Corner House at Annfield Plain. This was a free show and was enormously patronized. Trapeze work was generally a speciality and there were many imitations by the lads of the place, not infrequently with danger to life and limb.

As no charge was made for witnessing the performances the proprietor recouped his costs by the sale of hardware etc, and by the sale of lottery tickets at 6d each. Prizes of various kinds of hardware, flash jewellery, etc were drawn for. This mode of business no doubt paid as Carter travelled the colliery districts of Durham for many years. Other periodic events were the Kyo Flower Show Day, Durham Gala Day, Store Tea Day and visits by Hoffman's Concert Party from Newcastle.

In addition there were Professor Morgan the mesmeriser and Alexander Blythe (Secretary of the Miners' Permanent Relief Fund) with his Magic Lantern Show. Concerts, penny readings, etc, were also organized by the religous bodies who all seemed to want to cater for the leisure and enjoyment of the people. There seemed to be more satisfaction and pleasure and contentment from these than from our present day amusements, and at considerably less cost.

This description of a typical mining village could have applied to dozens of communities throughout Northumberland and Durham.

4 The Dying Breed

Now, in the last decade of the twentieth century my thoughts go back to the thousands of mining people who were born in the first decade, and had no choice in their selection of a working career.

After reaching the age to start work, normally fourteen, the son would leave school on the Friday, and he would go with his father to see the colliery manager on the Saturday. He would start underground on the following Monday. It was the expected thing that the sons followed their fathers down the pit, or the colliery manager wanted to know the reason why. With the families living in a tied colliery house the father had no option.

The girls after leaving school would have to remain at home to help their mothers, unless they were lucky enough to obtain a place in service with one of the local professional families in the village. The children leaving school at this time would have received a rudimentary form of education (the 3 Rs), and with money in short supply the bright children had to forego any chance of further eduation. Only a very small number were fortunate enough to take up the higher levels of learning.

The following interviews are with people born at the beginning of the

The hard days - Waldridge Fell miners during the General Strike *(Pelton Fell Action Group)*

century who actually worked in the times which were described previously. Their generation is coming to the end of its days. These are the last of a special breed of people, who never will be surpassed. Unfortunately they are becoming "The Dying Breed".

HERBIE LOGAN

MINER (BORN APRIL 1907)

I was born in a small village near Annfield Plain called Harelaw. I went to Harelaw School from the age of four until we moved to Greencroft and then I went to Catchgate School until I was 14. The reason I didn't continue - this is my reason - is that we weren't in very good circumstances at home and somebody had to work. Not liking to push myself forward, I went to work to let my brother go to school. That's actually what happened and I started work when I was 14 years of age at the Morrison North Pit.

Before that I had worked a little while as a Barber's assistant, but the work didn't appeal to me. I would sooner be at the Pit, so I started at the Pit when I was just turned 14 and I continued with the Pit right up to my retirement.

I started at the Morrison North Pit before the 1926 strike and I continued there until they got tired of paying us a wage. The wage then was 14s-l0d a week and that was after, I think it was half a crown or 2s-5d, off takes. That will leave, if you take the ratio between that and the wage that I took, the off takes was out of proportion to the wage they paid you, but however I got finished altogether. Now what was I to do? I either had to live on my mother and me brother- me father had died - and there was only me mother and she didn't want me to go away and me brother well he couldn't say much- it wasn't really up to him to say anything, but he was willing to keep us but I wasn't willing to stop so I went to London to find a job and I got a job as a cabinet maker. Not as a miner but as a cabinet maker.

I got home sick - I'll not tell you the reason I got home sick, but me mother wanted us back home, so back home I came, and I had no work. Just the dole, and it was a bit difficult to get the dole. They were not prepared to pay you for running away to London, but never mind I got over that little bit episode.

Just for the sake of me mother I had to have a job and it was easy to get for me because me brother was a gaffer. He had passed his first class manager's ticket and he got a better job at the Busty Pit, that's the

Morrison Busty Pit, Annfield Plain *(Mr Cozens, Sacriston)*

Morrison Busty. I was asked by my brother to start at the Morrison Busty Pit at Annfield Plain and I said 'No. I have a mate working at Tanfield Lea who will speak for me for a job'. So I went to see me old mate. He was working at the blackin' factory at Tanfield Lea. I says 'Can you get me on?' and he says, 'Aye , come down and see Mr say- an'- say', I just forget his name, and he says ' Tell him I sent you down for a start'. So I went and he says 'Aye, ye can start at the pit tomorrow'. I says 'Righto'. So back home I went and said, 'Get my pit clothes out I'm starting work again'.

'Where ?'

'Tanfield Lea'.

'How are you going to get there?'

'Well, if our lad will not lend us his bike I'll walk it'.

Anyway, I got there and I was there I tell you about four year. I used to walk from Greencroft to Tanfield Lea and it's a distance of about three mile ye naa, and I had to walk back an' all if the shift was wrong. I never asked for a change of shift and I remember it was a penny from Stanley down to Tanfield Lea in the bus, the Northern bus. The fare was one penny, and from Greencroft to Stanley it was four pence return, that was tuppence each way. That was all the bus fares it cost you. I think I had about fifteen shilling a week pay.

'What were you doing at Tanfield - coal hewing ? '

No I wasn't, not in the beginning, I was just on datal. You got more money, especially if you were in with a good set, and I thank the Lord to this day for the lads that I worked with at Tanfield Lea. They're the best in the world they are. Yes, I don't like to mention names but there was some great lads. They would help you and they were in the blackin' factory the same as me, but there was money to be made in the pit if you were willing to work, and I would work, so they took us on

I could never come up to me brother's wage though ye naa, but I used to say to me mother, 'Well that's all there is'. I still got me pocket money equivalent to the wage I earned. I didn't get any more. I would have to ask her if I wanted anything else, and it was always 'What do you want it for?' and I had to have a good excuse or I didn't get it. I enjoyed Tanfield Lea that much and the men that I worked with that it was in my mind not to move, but it was me mother. She says 'It'll save yis walking'. Mind it was a long walk every day and then walking back, and I says 'No, Right', and I wouldn't disappoint her, so that's how I came back, else I dont't think I would have come back, I would have stayed at Tanfield Lea, a grand pit. I always talk about the pit, but it was a good pit.

'That was the Margaret ?'

Yes the Margaret, the one that got the bad name, bad conditions. They weren't, they were excellent, but you had to work. You couldn't de it for nothing. So I divn't know whether that's right or wrong but you got nothing out of Robinson unless you worked for it.

'He was the Manager ?'

George Robinson was the Manager, and you didn't get anything, and I didn't blame him. We just did the ordinary work that the lads did, always. That was always enough. After pressure from me mother I decided to move to the Morrison Busty.

'How long were you at the Morrison Busty?'

Twenty years. It was something I'd never seen before, all these ropes, and tubs and forks. I'd never seen anything like that in the mine. It was all foreign. I says well this is a magnificent pit, anybody would like to work here. But it was home from home, and a good set of men, and that's all the difference between a good pit and a bad pit, it's the men that ye work with.

'You are at the Morrison Busty now and you're driving a hauler ?'

I did drive a hauler. I didn't like it. I says, 'I want to be oot there amang the lads, I didn't want to de all this'. Anyway, it followed on from that. Our lad says, 'Now, it's about time you had your Deputy's ticket isn't it ?'.

Well, I knew a man, well the whole family knew him, Vernon Richards, he used to come to the house. He says, 'I'm starting a class. It'll not be any use to you, but you've got to have your name on so that you can apply for permission to sit the examination, but for what you'll learn, I cannot learn you it, you're far too far in front of me, but you've got to have your name on this for to sit the examination'.

'Righto', I says. This is where I has to call him Mr. Richards. 'Righto, Mr. Richards, I'll be down'. I was in the room where we assembled for the very first time. I felt a hand touch us and I just put me hand doon, and a half- a-crown was put in, 2/6d, the old half crown. Mr. Ward the headmaster give us it to pay me fee. I says to meself, ' Oh, champion, I've already gettin' half-a-crown off me mother, I'll pay me fee and I'll gan and have a game of billiards with Mr Ward'. Ay, the things ye've done. Money was nowt in them days. It was very, very small money.

Talkin' about playing billiards, I wouldn't dare. At the Miners' Hall at New Kyo it was one penny for a game of billiards. The Store Hall was a little bit dearer, it was three ha'pence. When you came down the big hall, Riley's, well it was business, it was tuppence. There was a big difference between a penny and tuppence - you got twice as much billiards at the Miners' Hall.

'You passed your Deputy's Ticket then?'

Aye, it was neither nowt nor something. I just kept on. I used to like the men and I says I'm stopping on piecework. It was only I got taked off it to be a Deputy. I wouldna have been a one. They said, 'Well you've sat your ticket', but I says, 'I divn't care. I'd rather not'. He says, 'Why, you see you must think of the others. Your brother's a gaffer and if you stop on the way you are and any stories get repeated . . .'

'Why not likely', I says, 'The men wouldnt do that, not the men I know'.

'You don't know men', he says, 'They're ever carrying the tale between one and the other'.

'OK, I'll de what you want then', I says. So I had to gan up and see the boss and I started Deputy work. I'm a little bit dim in the memory about that, whether it was just before the war or just after the war that I started.

My brother decided to move. 'I don't know whether that's right,' I said. I thought he should have stopped, but he wanted to move, so he left and applied for a job at Tanfield Lea. Not at the Margaret mind, but what is it ye call the other pit? East Tanfield, a dirty, wet place. He went there, and I says, 'Ye mug, leaving a pit like this'. That was the Busty, but it was an advancement to him. He moved on, and later he got both the pits at

Tanfield, and then he got the next pit to it, further over, I forget the names now. Then he got a General Manager's job - he had four or five pit.

'So you finally retired from the Morrison Busty, and you would have been a Union member all those years ?'

Oh, all them years I was in the Union, paid the Union every fortnight for all the time. Never, never missed.

'When did you finally retire ?'

When I was 65, in 1974.

GEORGE (ABE) WALES

BORN AT ANNFIELD PLAIN IN 1909

I was born into a family of thirteen, eight boys and five girls. At the age of twelve years old, I gave the mine manager at Neasham Drift at Iveston a false age and started working down the mine at twelve years instead of the legal age of fourteen. I worked along with another boy, water leading. That is trying to keep the drift mine and its work places dry by transporting the water in a water tub out of the drift to bank. I worked seven twelve hour shifts at my age for a weekly wage of £2-12s-6d. As it happened I was the biggest wage earner in the family, because at that time my father who was a coal hewer at the Morrison Busty at Annfield Plain was below me in his earnings.

I worked at this mine until I was fourteen years of age and with a new birth certificate, I went to the Morrison North Pit and started work legally. I stayed at this pit for two years until I was sixteen, when hearing that I could make 2s-6d a week more at the Medomsley Busty in the Main Coal Seam doing the job of hand putting. Which was pushing the tubs from the coal face by hand not using a pit pony.

The next step in my mining journey was at the age of twenty two, I moved back to the Morrison North Pit, I did not stay very long before I moved on to the Eden Colliery (for more money) situated near the Jolly Drovers Pub at Leadgate. My job at the Eden was using one of the first coal cutters in the country. It was driven by compressed air and was made by British Jeffery Diamond. The cutter was used as a short wall machine making roadways and headings.

The seam was twenty one inches thick in that particular district. You had to cut sufficient coal out to allow the stone to be packed in its place. This meant that no stone was sent to bank. The problem with this machine at this time in 1932 was that you had to keep stopping it after an hours work to defrost it.

Regarding the union of which I was always a paid up member, I took part in the 1921 and the 1926 national strikes It was during the 1926 strike when the Eden Colliery Management (Consett Iron Company) locked their miners out. They then began to employ people from the south west of Durham, places like Hunwick, High Grange, and Woodhouse to take the place of the locals. These people had to be housed, so Consett Iron Company began to build bungalows at Delves Lane, Pont Street and Watling Street to house these strangers.

Low Pit, Pelton Colliery *(Pelton Fell Action Group)*

At the end of the strike when some of the old Eden men were allowed back there was a stampede to start again, but a lot of the jobs had already been taken by what was, at that particular time, strangers. That was the Manager's excuse to keep out who he didn't want.

During the 1926 strike my family managed very well. My father who never drank in his life and had never set foot in a picture house was a gardener with large garth (allotment) at Stoney Heap, providing the household with all the fresh vegetables it required. As there were seven miners in the family out on strike we hit upon a money making idea. On the Fell between Stoney Heap and the Eden Colliery one of the shallow coal seams could be worked because it was only six feet below the surface. My brothers and I had a successful business going during the duration of the strike.

I went up to the pit to see the manager when things had started up again and Mr. Harper (a nice fellow) asked me what I wanted. I replied, 'A start'. The mining union secretary was present and he said, 'You can't start Abe, because you have knocked other men back'.

'I can start who I want', the Manager replied and offered me a job to start work at the Eden that very night. I refused his offer because I was doing alright with my fiddling jobs.

I did start at the Eden after a while and worked on development work opening out new districts at the Stoney Heap end of the colliery. The old pit which was situated near the Jolly Drovers was coming to the end of its life and production was being started up at Stoney Heap.

At this time the family, all fourteen of us, were living in a two bedroomed house at Stoney Heap. The little bed room had two beds for my four sisters and the two smallest boys. My mam and my dad slept in the front room downstairs, and the rest of us had to sleep anywhere we could. As I was my mother's pet (and the main wage earner) I got the job of being door man. With my brothers and sisters coming in late from the pictures and Castles (dance hall) at the weekend, and with only one key, my mother used to shout 'Abe, open the door and let them in'. I was so mad at being woken up so many times that the next day I took a screw driver and took all the locks and bolts off the front and back doors. So they could come and go any time during the twenty four hours.

My mother must have been the most hard working woman in the world. No matter what time my father or my brothers (nine of us) came in from the pit a dinner would be ready for us waiting on the table. So with all the meal times and having to put nine baits up for us to go to work plus all the other household jobs she had no time for anything but work. She worked a twenty four hour shift seven days a week. She was a very remarkable woman. Whatever time my father had away from the pit, he spent it growing vegetables in his many allotments. He also kept hens and pigs and his only luxury was his pipe. He loved to smoke his pipe.

After the War I was still working at the Eden. I had a wandering job between the old pit and Stoney Heap. I was looking after conveyors and other machines. In 1956 I received a fractured spine caused by a fall of stone. This brought my mining days to an end. I still receive a disability pension for this. So my mining career was at:

Neasham Drift

Iveston

Morrison North Pit

Busty Main Coal, Medomsley

Tantobie

Morrison Busty New Pit

Then to the Eden Colliery - the main one.

My pit days were over but my working days continued. I obtained a small holding, in the Wear Valley at Frosterley which I worked successfully. One day, while out walking, I called in at a nearby Lead Mine (of which there were many in the valley). I found that the generator had broken down. I popped my head in the door and asked the men what was the trouble. A man, who I later found out was the manager, replied, 'The mine is at a standstill because nobody can mend the generator'.

'I'm handy with machines, can I have a go?' I said.

In half an hour the machine was running and the mine was back to work. The manager asked me my name and where I lived and then he offered me the job of maintenance man. This suited me exactly. My small holding was nearby, so working both jobs I made money.

Unfortunately I had to leave the farm, and so I retired to live at Greencroft. Then I started a small transport buisness with my son. As my health did not improve I again retired and moved into a old people's bungalow at Annfield Plain and I am quite happy.

TOM FRENCH

BORN AT ASHINGTON IN 1905

My family moved into the area and I went to the local school until I was fourteen years of age. After leaving school I started work at the Moor Pit (Harelaw), and later moved to the Bog Drift at Ravenside. I was driving with a pony and at the men's bait time, I had, along with my friend John Chesterfield, penned (filled up the holes between the rails with stones) before the other set of driver lads were due to start. Instead of doing all the penning we used to go inbye to have a chat with the coal hewers. This particular morning I said to my friend John , 'John, I am going outbye'.

'I'm stopping in, Tom', he said.

'Pinky (Mr Pinkney the overman) will be coming in, so watch yourself ', I said, and away I went outbye. As I was going out I bumped into Pinky, who said, 'What are you doing, Tommy?'

'I'm doing nowt', I said. He went further inbye and met my mate John and

Dipton (Old Delight) *(supplied by the author)*

asked him, 'What are you doing John?'

'Well, I'm helping Tommy.'

'Helping Tommy? But he's doing nowt'

So when the overman went to the drift mouth cabin to meet the back shift men he said, 'Aye lads, listen to this I've heard the best ioke of the year. There's a bloke inbye doing nowt and his marra is helping him.'

Mr Pinkney who was a decent fellow used to send me down to his house at Catchgate every morning to collect his bait from his wife. I always got a banana from her for doing this job.

When I left the Bog Drift I got work at the New Delight Pit at Dipton, and while I was there I was a pony putter and then started to hand hew.

After a while I had the chance of a start at East Tanfield Colliery for better money. The money for working forty or forty five hours a week was £2-5s-0d per week. It was a terrible place, very wet and the management provided no protective clothing. The work was very hard hewing and if you didn't make it you would not be paid for it. The money averaged out at two pounds a week, whilst the County Average was thirty six shillings (£1.80). I didn't like it so I looked for another move. I moved to Friarside Drift which was in the valley below the Lintz Colliery. This was a good move for me for there was a chance to make more money. I hewed in the

Townley and the Tilley Seams and was happy to remain there for a while. Unfortunately the drift closed and I was on the move again. This time I ended up at the Hobson Colliery (Burnopfield).

My job at the Hobson was special work. That means back bye work (setting girders, making bore holes). It was all hard going. Our wages for this work were reasonable. At that time we were using hand picks, later they started to put in windy diggers (pneumatic picks), so I started using them. The man demonstrating the new picks was a great friend of mine, who lived at Annfield Plain. I did a little practice with him and I became a little good un at the game. I was a good coal digger and I made a lot of money. We also used the windy drillers, which were very heavy for a little fella like me. I am only five feet one inches in height and my weight is nine and a half stone. My work was setting twelve foot H girders on my own, also 9' by 7' arch girders. It showed that a good little un was as good as a big un down the pit.

One of my old East Tanfield friends had a bit of a difference with the gaffer, and he left and went to work at the Morrison North Pit at Annfield Plain. He said to me 'Tommy if you come over to the Morrison, I will get you a start'.

I thought long and hard, then I decided to give it a try as I was always working night shift. When I went to the North Pit on the Monday morning, I got into the pit yard, stopped and said to myself, 'I don't take

"Back shift riding"

to this place'. So I turned around and went back home. On the Friday the Morrison North Pit exploded and twenty one miners lost their lives. Among them was my friend. Someone up there was looking after me.

I was a National Union of Mineworkers member from 1919 until I retired in 1969. That was fifty years a member and I took part in two national strikes. My reward for my service was a presentation at the Travellers Rest at Burnopfield (the Newcastle footballer Jack Allan's pub). I received seven pint cheques for free beer and a pound off 'The Durham Miners Association' for fifty years at the pit, also a plaque, and the plaque went into the coal house.

The end of my mining days, did not mean the end of my working days. Since leaving the pit my jobs have been: a lollipop man, a club doorman, and a club steward. One day while I was taking the dog out for a walk, I was passing the Engineering Factory at Leadgate. I asked the gaffer for a start. He said, 'Can you make tea?'

I said, 'Yes', and I was there as tea boy for fifteen years. I really enjoyed working there but I had to retire from this post when I reached the age of eighty five. I miss it very much, and I am looking for another job.

BETTY FRENCH

BORN TANTOBIE, 1912.

Tommy and I were married on the 18th of July 1931 at Tantobie Church and we lived in with my mother at Bellerby's Buildings, Tantobie.

We had a baby (a boy) we called him Sammy and when Tommy unfortunately came out of work and had to go on the dole we received about twenty one shillings (£1.05) a week to keep the three of us. And you never knew when the Means Test Man was at your door. He never knocked, he just banged in straight up to you and looked around, and if you were lucky enough to have anything good on your table he would wonder where you got the money for it. If you were on the dole for so long, you could go on to parish relief. Then you had to go to this local chap, a very nasty chap to claim your relief. He gave you a little slip of paper and all you could get was margarine, flour and yeast, just the main things. You got no luxuries because times were hard. I think it was about eight shillings (40p) a week. That was in 1932.

Fortunately Tommy got work again, but they were on short time. Then there was a slump in the collieries up until war was declared when they opened up the old collieries and that's when the miners got full time work. This lasted until the end of the war and in 1947 the Labour Government nationalised the pits. This was a great thing to happen for the miners. Their wages increased under the National Coal Board because under privatisation (that was the Bowes Lyons and their friends) the wage was very, very poor and the men had to work for their money. If they did not get their share of coal, they did not get paid. They were on the minimum wage which was £1-l0s-0d to £1-12s-0d per week. If they had a good week the wage was £2-l0s-0d. They worked damned hard for it. My husband used to come in and I used to be up through the night to dry his clothes and then dash the clothes against the wall outside to get all the dust out of them for him to return to the colliery the next day. It was really slavish work. Now it is reasonable, but then it was slavery.

In my younger days the strikes were in progress and we could hardly get fed at home because we were getting no money with the husbands and fathers being on strike. We got no money, maybe just a little bit of Relief for the mothers and the children but this was very, very small, so they set up Soup Kitchens in the nearest place. Well, I lived at Tantobie and we had to travel to Tanfield Lea. There was no buses, we had to walk there, with maybe holes in our shoes because we couldn't afford them, and cast-offs from our elders and, what's never known today, patches on the boys trousers. We used to go straight down to the Chapel to have a thick hot chocolate, cocoa, and a thick slice of bread and jam, come back and do our lessons. In the dinner hour we used to go straight back to the Soup Kitchens for a bowl of thick hot broth, and another slice of bread and also a cup of hot cocoa again - thick, you could cut it with a knife! Then again back to school to do our lessons. That was in the hard days, and that went on a very long time and very frequently. As the strikes were very often we got nothing and it was very hard times. No new shoes, all cast-offs, if a neighbour helped out. That was the way. We all helped each other those days.

When I was fifteen I was asked to play the piano at Tantobie Club. The event was the annual trip of the North Shields fish wives. This started my piano playing career and I am still playing today in a little pub in the village of Medomsley. A total career up to the present of 65 years.

During our married life Tommy and I have moved house ten times. I think I will settle down in this one, which is an Aged Miners Cottage at Leadgate. Tommy who is out of work is a little upset because he can only go out to the pub six nights a week.

MARY WALES (LEE)

BORN, HOWDON-LE-WEAR, 1912

I was born at High Grange, Howdon-Le-Wear, Bishop Auckland. I was the youngest of a family of six - four sisters and one brother, Bill. With my parents this made eight living in the house. When they were old enough, my four sisters entered service, out of the district. As I was the youngest I had to stay home to look after my Mam and Dad.

My father, Thomas Lee, was a miner at Roughly Colliery, Hunwick. He unfortunately died in 1929 at the age of 64. This left my Mother and I to exist on her widow's pension of 10 shillings (50p) a week. As the house rent was 6s 10d (34p) per week this left us 3s 2d (16p) to live on. Naturally I had to find some kind of work to help out, and I found a job at Mrs. Snowden's farm at High Grange. The work was in the fields; potato picking, turnip cutting and when the harvest time arrived I worked on the threshing machine and hay making. As I was handy with needle and thread Mrs Snowden had me mending her wool stockings and other needlework. For this work I was paid 2s 6d (12.5p) per week. This made a total of 5s 8d (28p) for Mam and I to live on.

At the outbreak of war in 1914 my brother Bill ran away and volunteered for the Durham Light Infantry at the age of sixteen. When my parents tracked him down to bring him home, he pleaded with them to be allowed to stay, as he would be called up when he was eighteen. Reluctantly they agreed to do this and he was one of the unfortunate ones to be gassed during his service. When he returned home the pit at Roughly was doing very bad so he had to find a job elsewere. Owing to the gassing he received, he was unable to do any coal hewing, so he found a job at Eden Colliery, Leadgate as a pump attendant. He lived at Delves Lane in a colliery house where he died at the age of 52.

When my Father was alive and working at the pit, no matter what time he arrived home there would be a large dinner awaiting him. His favourite meal at that time was onion or leek puddings. Like all miners' wives at that time my Mother was very organised. There was certain days for certain jobs and the week would be organised like this:

Monday - Brushing and pressing the Sunday Best and placing them in grease-proof paper in the press (chest of drawers) for the next Sabbath.

Tuesday - Washing day was the worst day of the week. The clothes were washed, scrubbed, washed and soaped, washed again, then starched, then hung on an outside line to dry.

Wednesday - Iron the clothes that were washed the previous day, then put them to air on a line inside the house.

Thursday - Put away the washing and then start to bake for the week (bread, teacakes, pies, and cakes).

Friday - Clean the house right through, black lead the fire place and fire irons and clean the brasses.

Saturday - Clean the front room, set the fire for the day following which was the Sabbath. A clean proggy mat would be put on the floor in front of the fire.

Sunday - In my time at home this was always recognised as a day of rest. Nothing would be done. The knitting and sewing jobs had to lie untouched as this was the Sabbath Day, a day of prayer and rest. Every Sunday morning we would walk to the Methodist Chapel at Bitchburn. On Sunday evening the family went for a walk in the neighbourhood which was the done thing at that time. After walking we returned home and took off our best clothes ready for the Monday chores. Coming home from our walk we would sit in the front room, have a cup of tea and a chat then go to bed. The system started over again the next day.

My brother Bill working at Leadgate brought his new friend to meet us at home, this was the begining of my very happy life with George. We were married at Hunwick Parish Church in 1936. We obtained a house in Chirnside Terrace, New Greencroft, Annfield Plain. George retained his job as a miner at the Eden Colliery.

At that time life was very hard. We had started a family and our weekly income was £1-18s-0d (£1.90) a week. Out of this the rent for our house was 13 shillings (65p) per week so we had to look twice before we bought anything owing to having little money. We raised four children (three boys and one girl) and after struggling with little money we remained a very happy family.

If we live until the 1st of August 1992 we will have been married 56 years. My only wish would be that George's health would improve.

MARGARET KOZDEN (MACINTOSH)

BORN, GLASGOW, 1919

The family moved to England when I was three months old, and we lived in 'Spice Cake Row', which was Robson's Terrace, Flint Hill. My father was a miner and he worked at the Lintz Colliery, Burnopfield. Unfortunately he died at the age of 42. It was then the hard times started for my mother.

I was the youngest child of four, two sisters and a brother, so my mother had a hard task to bring the family up. I can remember the Relief Officers coming to our house to inspect my mother's effects. She had a press which she had bought with a struggle from Hardy's Shop at Stanley. They told her she must sell this and live on the proceeds before they could give her any help. My brother found a job in a local brickworks, so he had to leave home. If there was a wage coming in they would stop your relief money. Eventually he emigrated, along with other men from Dipton, to Canada.

During one of the many strikes around at that time I can remember going to school where I met the parish priest Father Leary who had three pairs of boots to hand out. He said to me, 'What size do you take Maggie?' I hated that man for offering me charity, but I had no shoes so I had to swallow my pride and accept a pair.

The problem was that when you were 'on the relief' you had to be very careful what you put on the table, because these relief officers would just walk into your home unannounced and if they found anything which they considered a luxury they demanded to know where you'd obtained the money to buy it.

The local policeman was called Mr Callender and I was frightened to death of him. I did not like going to school, so this day my elder sister dragged me along to his home, and he gave me a lecture about not going to school. He frightened me so much, I never played the 'Nick' again. When I left school I had many jobs. One was at the St Vincent de Paul's home in Newcastle, but my mother took ill and I had to leave this job to nurse her. When I returned home I found no food in the house, so I went to church and prayed for help. I then went to the Relief Office which was situated opposite the libary at Catchgate. The officers' names were Mr Brass and Mr Jeffery. These men, along with other men, questioned me on why I was there. I explained the reason and after a while they granted me a voucher which would obtain for me a gill (0.14 litres) of milk and one egg per day. I was so excited on having been granted this I ran all the way from Catchgate to Flint Hill to tell my mother.

My mother always managed to put a meal on the table for me and my sisters. I will never understand how she did it. The regular things would be herrings, potatoes, cabbage, in any order. Herrings could be bought twenty for a penny so they were regular. It was my job to clean them, and my sisters conned me into thinking I was the best cook in the house so I got that job. In fact I baked from the age of ten: white bread, brown bread, tea cakes. Anything which would fill you up.

People talk about the good old days, but the only good thing about them was that people were kinder to each other, and they rallied round to help. I think it was because everyone was in the same boat - Poor.

The local angel was Mrs Robson who lived in Sawmill Buildings. Every village had one at that time. She was midwife, undertaker and all problems you took to her. It was a question of the poor looking after each other.

The miners received their house coal in one ton loads, and one of my many tasks was to go around the streets and offer to put in the coals for anybody who would give me six bucketfuls for my mother, as she was not receiving any.

Then came the war years. There were hard and bad times before this, but they became worse with rationing. My neighbour Mrs Carter and I used to share everything. We had one chip pan between us as we could not get enough dripping to have one each.

All the vegetables were halved between us to try and manage. By the end of the war I was married and had a family of three - two boys and a daughter. The flat where we lived had no hot water or bathroom, so my husband and I plus the children had to bathe in a tin bath and when we were finished I would wash the clothes in what remained of the hot water.

My rations during the war I bought at the Co-op at Dipton, and with the dividend running at two shilling in the pound (10%), I would hope to buy shoes for the bairns at the end of the quarter (Dividend Day). If I had not enough money it meant another cardboard sole for the shoes. The biggest help to me was the school jumble sales. I owned an old treadle sewing machine and being good with my hands, I could turn any clothes I obtained at the jumble sale into very good clothes for my daughter. In fact she was one of the best dressed girls at St Patrick's school at that time. I also made print dresses into pillow cases, and I must have had the bonniest pillow cases in Durham. They lasted for years.

INTERVIEWS - CONCLUSIONS

The one thing I found in interviewing the people who make up this section of the book is their determination. Determination, not to succeed, but to survive. They have a great deal in common having survived the 1920s and 1930s, working in the conditions the men were expected to. Everything after that had to be a bonus for them. The wives were also employed on a twenty four hour basis - if they were not cooking and drying the pit clothes they would have been planning, wondering what to put on the table, and also how to escape the clutches of the dreaded Means Test.

Margaret summed it up when she said the 'working people rallied round to help each other because everyone of them was in the same boat - Poor!' While the two world wars were dreadful affairs, the one good thing that comes out of a war is full employment, and after the Second World War was over and a Labour Government was returned the first good fortune to come the miner's way happened - nationalisation of the coal mines.

This changed the miner's status from one of near slavery to one of a man who had a purpose in life. Money improved and working conditions dramatically took a turn for the better. The work was still very dangerous but the safety standards improved considerably.

Even when the National Coal Board took over in 1947 there were still problems between Management and the Unions but the living conditions improved beyond belief. At the present time the men in my story all have different circumstances regarding their health. Tommy French was finally forced into retirement last year at the age of 86 and is looking for a job. Herbie is in a nursing home until his health improves.

Abe is in poor health but is wonderfully nursed by his loving wife Mary. Betty French and Margaret are still very active, Betty still playing the piano and Margaret doing charity work - she has a very busy agenda.

The one thing that stands out in these people is their cheerful attitude to life. It is amazing to the majority of the young generation how people can experience the conditions and hardship which this generation lived through. It puts them into a very special category which I expect will not be surpassed. It makes one feel very humble and even angry to listen to them and to record their stories. These people and many like them in the North East are very special and we should not forget them.

5 Industrial Relations - Managers and Miners

The man installed in the job of colliery manager was required to have obtained a 1st class or 2nd class manager's certificate. He was appointed by the coal owners to oversee the day to day working of the colliery and to sort out the many problems which would arise during the working of the pit. He would live near the colliery in a large house with spacious lawns and gardens and probably have a retired miner tending them for him.

The colliery manager before nationalisation would usually be of the same religious persuasion as the owner and many of them in County Durham followed the Methodist faith. Usually he would have been a Justice of the Peace, or Magistrate, so any miner summoned to court for some petty problem would be confronted by his colliery manager. He would sit in his office, master of all he surveyed. Lord and Master of the miners working for him, and their families. Not only had he to run the pit at a profit he had to be mentor, adviser, judge and jury to the miner and his family. On a whim he could end or mend the livelihood of any man brought before him.

A series of minutes have been assembled regarding deputations made to management by miners and their union officials. It will show the power the manager could wield over his miners. The minutes are factual and the deputations took place at South Medomsley Colliery, Dipton between the years 1918— 1923.

DEPUTATION - 23rd April 19?

PRESENT:

MANAGEMENT

?

WORKMEN

H. Kirk	(Check Weighman and Union Secretary)
T. Houghton	Miner
P. Fox	Miner

The men asked that the buzzer be blown more regularly.

P. Fox stated that 10 watches were put together and the men got 3 minutes difference the next day

This was disputed by the management and they asked for the names of the people concerned. The men refused.

The management contended that some boys were persistently late-comers, and this must stop. They also promised that attention would be given to the buzzer.

The men requested that men coming to the shaft bottom in a very wet condition be allowed to "ride" first. This was agreed.

DEPUTATION - 20th August 1918

PRESENT:

MANAGEMENT

J.T. Robinson	Manager
P. Bolam	Under Manager

WORKMEN

H. Kirk	Check Weighman and Union Secretary
J. Pearce	
M. Laverick	
W. Hogg	

The men asked management to provide a 'men seat' to transport the men from the shaft bottom to their place of work, for both the foreshift and the backshift. The men explained that with a 'ride inbye' they would be fitter to hew coal, as the distance could be 2-3 miles. They promised to hew one extra tub of coal if this could be arranged. If transport was not available the men would walk inbye.

The management agreed to the backshift men having a ride at the appropriate times agreed to.

After discussion it was agreed that the question of riding on the foreshift be deferred to a later date.

DEPUTATION - 30th Octoher 1918

PRESENT:

MANAGEMENT

J.T. Robinson	Manager

WORKMEN

H. Kirk	Check Weighman and Union Secretary
Foster	Miner
Morland	Miner
J. Hcdson	Miner

The case of the dismissal of John Howe was discussed. It appears that John Howe used bad language in a colliery house where a corpse was lying, and also to the woman in attendance.

If the management would not withdraw the fourteen days' notice of his dismissal, the men would 'stop the pit'.

In his defence, John Howe stated that he was drurk, having consumed 7 glasses of gin in 25 minutes; he did not know what he had done.

After discussion, management agreed to withdraw his notice.

DEPUTATION ON EXPOSIVES

27th July 1920

PRESENT:

MANAGEMENT

J.T. Robinson	Manager
J. Davies	Manager's Clerk
P. Bolam	Under Manager

WORKMEN

H. Kirk	Check Weighman and Union Secretary
T. Oughton	Miner
W. Hogg	Miner
R. Reed	

The men stated that the powder which they bought from management was unable to 'shoot the caunch'.

[The caunch was the stone which was left when the coal had been extracted, e.g. if the height of the coal tub was 4 feet, the height of the coal 2 feet, this left 2 feet of stone (the caunch) to be removed by explosives.]

The men asked the management to provide them with 'rip' [a more modern type of explosive in stick form, but more expensive].

The management promised the men that 'rip' would be supplied to hewers when the hardness of the stone warranted, but if 'powder' can do the work, it must be used as required by the Inspector of Mines.

DEPUTATION

11th September 1921

Breach of Coal Mine Regulations

Present

Management

J.T.Robinson	Manager
J.Davis	Clerk
C.Musgrove	Overman

Workers

P.Barrett	Miner
Jack Graham	Miner

Trespasses

Men must take proper travelling arrangements. Men must each give their tokens to the signalman (banksman) or hang it on the nail provided. Proceedings will be taken for any breach of these rules.

Powder Tins

When marra's change, they must have their own powder tins (to carry explosives), and the box must be stamped with his token number.

William Foster has come out by the travelling way and sent his token out by another man, and he has done this again since he was cautioned. Any repetition he will be prosecuted without further caution.

J.Beverly, T.Fazackerly and J. Emberson were reported by the Government Inspector Mr Cummings on 9-9-1922 for breaking the timber rules.

DEPUTATION

1st March 1923

Minimum Wage Deputation

Present

Management

Workers

W.Morland	Miner
P.Barrett	Miner
R.Tennant	Miner

It was stated that marras Tennant and English had earned.

3rd pay 2nd week 6s-6d per shift

4th pay 1st week 7s-4d per shift

4th pay 2nd week 7s-2d per shift

Tennant and English had reported to W. Nicholson (Deputy) on 21st Febuary 1923.

They reported to C.Musgrove (Overman) on 23rd Febuary 1923.

The miners complained that they had not been paid the wages for which they worked.

They claimed that on Monday 26th Febuary Mick English could not get into his cavil for Stythe (Foul Air) and he filled 16 tubs out of Bordy's place (Cavil) and Mossom filled 16 tubs out of the same place. I got into my own place and filled only 6 tubs because I could not see where I was working.

Management replied that they will be paid consideration for the Monday for working in bad air, but will pay nothing for the Minimum Wage as full time has not been worked.

6 Appendix

A selection of accounts and wage bills which were a financial record of the many mining interests during the years on Pontop Pike.

In 1823 came the first indication that coke was being made at the pit heads on Pontop Pike, with an account of 2s-4d being paid to someone for working one day at the "Sunder Oven".

There was obviously a sort of apprenticeship system in operation for some of the trades at the pits. In 1799 for example, the son of a Mr. Hunter of White-le-head bound himself for 3 years "to be instructed and learn the art of waggonway wright and to attend or work at any waggonway above or below ground".He was to be paid 10d per day for the first year, 12d per day for the second and 14d per day for the third.

Mr. Nicholson of Dipton bound himself on similar terms "to attend any machine or engine as banksman" and "to carry out any necessary jobs or repairs" or "any other work which the owners require when the pits are idle at Christmas".

The following is the "waling and shaling" account at the Pontop Pike Colliery dated 8th of December to 22nd of December 1786. It will be interesting to note that both boys and girls were employed at the work.

		£	s	d
Mathew Anderson	12 days at 10d		10	0
Isabella Oswell	11 days at 6d		5	6
Ann Robinson	4 days at 4d		1	4
Sarah Irwin	8 days at 6d		4	0
Mary Naisby	4 days at 6d		2	0
Roger Oxley	9 days at 10d		7	6
Ann Robinson	3 days at 4d		1	0

It is interesting to compare the cost of living in the late 19th century to the wages paid to the miners at that time.

1 lb of Tea	2s-0d
1 lb of Sugar	2d
1 lb of Rice	2d
1 lb of Coffee	ls-8d
1 lb of Dutch Cheese	6d
1 lb of Currants	4d
Tin of Salmon	8d
A pair of pit boots	5s-4d
Apair of women's shoes	4s-0d

In 1767 Pontop Colliery was reported to have an annual vend of 50,000 chaldrons a year, or 150,000 tons. The neighbouring Silvertop Colliery yielded 20,000 chaldrons, or 60,000 tons annually.

A typical wage bill of a Pontop Pike colliery about this time was.-

Hewing Account.

	£	s	d
Hewing 42 scores at 1s-l0d per score	3	17	0
Hewing 165 scores at 2s-0d per score	16	10	0
Making $41^1/_2$ yards of headings at 8d each	1	7	8
Making 15 yards of narrow work at 2d each		2	6
Hewing 24 scores and 10 corves of small coal at 2s-6d a score	3	1	3
Turning 7 bends at 9d each		5	3
Consideration for hard coal and troubles		5	2
TOTAL	25	8	10

Dividing the hewers' bill between the 30 hewers makes an average of 17s-5d per man.

There were 16 drivers, and their wages bill amounted to £16-3s-0d. They were paid 10d per day.

The overman was paid by piecework at $5^1/_2$d per score. As he accounted for 297 scores, his wages for 10 days amounted to £4-10s-6d.

There are many documents showing how closely mining was linked to agriculture in the early days.

Mr. Silvertop (one of the Ministeracres family) had mining interests at Bushblades, between Dipton and Harelaw, and one of his accounts refers to his mining and farming interests.-

13 pit lamps at 8d	
7 pokes at 18d	
31 yards of harn 7d	
* Ale for letting down horses	£1-3-6d
3 bolls of potatoes for pigs	2-0d
Gelding the pigs	1-6d
Oil for the gins	3-10d

There are payments dated about 1780 for "oats and old hay" and to William Brown for hoeing whins, but also payments to the overmen at the Broom and Venture pits for "working late at the boylers" and "repairs to the boylers".

** possibly the men looking after the horses were paid in kind , eg Ale.*

There are other accounts which give an idea how the pits were developing in the 19th century. They include accounts of money paid for the "saving of hundreds of sleepers", presumably for the waggonways, at 2s-6d per hundred. There are also miscellaneous items such as:

$2^1/_2$ days slitting deals at 2s-4d per day	5s-10d
4 days repairing pit houses at 2s-6d per day	10s-0d
1 day dressing head trees	2s-4d
2 days at Dunston Foundry getting waggon wheels	5s-0d
$^1/_2$ day mending "Hot Water Trows" at Lowd Pit	1s-2d
$^1/_2$ day mending screen at Delight Pit	1s-2d

2 days dressing and putting in rake shafts	4s-8d
1 day making a "Rowler for South Pit"	2s-4d
$1^1/_2$ days shovelling snow on the waggonway	3s-6d
$^1/_2$ day making cracketts	1s-2d

To give a comparison between prices and wages at this time (about 1830), the rents paid for mining families for their tied pit houses varied between 18s-0d and £1-15s-0d per year. It was a rule of the coal owners that if the father worked at a pit, he must make sure his sons followed him at the pit when they had come of age. So it was possible for a father and 2 - 6 sons living in the same house and working at the same pit.

The coal at this time was selling at prices ranging from 8s-0d to £1-0-0d per chaldon waggon (53cwts).

In 1763 a yearly bond was signed between the heirs of Lady Windsor and John Simpson of Bradley Hall, Ryton, owners of collieries on Pontop Pike, and their workpeople. It stipulated that:

> The parties hired shall continue at work without striking, combining or absenting themselves, shall deliver one corf (basket) of coal gratis every pay day (14 days).
>
> Shall be fined one shilling for every corf sent to bank (surface) less than full.
>
> Shall deliver to the owner one corf of coal gratis for every corf of coal set out (condemned for heavy stones among the coal).

On these conditions, coal hewers, drivers of sledge horses, drivers of gin horses, onsetters and banksmen bound themselves and each of their respective heirs and assigns in the penal sum of £18-10s-0d.

To this bond, which is stamped, the names of 110 hewers and 55 drivers all appear opposite seals.

The period of binding commenced on the 3rd of December 1763, and 6d per man was paid for the binding. The pits mentioned in this account of the Pontop Southside Waggonway, were owned by the East Pontop Coal Co, but the mineral rights were owned by the Marquis of Bute, who leased part of the royalty to the coal company.

The following is a contract between the proposed officials of the aforementioned pits and Mr. Fenwick of Collierley Dykes, Dipton, agent for the Marquis. It is dated 1797:

> We the undersigned agree to be set on at the Hive, Bogg and Success pits as overmen until Christmas at the price fixed.
>
> We promise to pay for or perform the following work:
>
> To pay onsetter, find oil and candles, keep the "Barroway" in good repair, and to work the pits using the "Long" way (that is taking all the coal).
>
> We promise to build stoppings or stone pillars three yards distance from each other.
>
> We agree to dress and cut all wooden pit props that may be used in working these pits, also to secure the roof by propping, also to set up a light every 40 yards and make *sure* every lamp is kept burning.

The coal hewers were to be made to dispose of the smallcoal, so it was not sent to bank to spoil the rest.

> We also promise not to work the coal ourselves, or work no other coal which is further up the pit.
>
> For any neglect we promise to pay two shillings from our earnings, and if we happen to go to work drunk, we agree to pay ten shillings and six pence for every such misdemeanour.

Signed	Hive Pit	-	*Abraham Bell*
	Bogg Pit	-	*William Richardson*
	Success Pit	-	*John Richardson*

N.B. This contract was typical of the times.

There were many agreements such as these between workmen and management, signed Mr. Fenwick (agent for the Marquis of Bute) at the office at CollierleyDykes.

1. Sink a stapple at the Success Pit for the counter-balance at the price of 20 pence per fathom. (dated 1797)
2. To drive a drift in the Hutton seam westward out of the Hive Pit workings. (1797)
3. To drive a bord from the Hive Pit towards Pontop west boundary to make a waggonway. (1797)
4. To drive a Brass Thill drift in the Success Pit to the top (shallow) seams southward. (1797)
5. To drive a drift in the Hutton seam at the Hive Pit at the rate of 15 pence per yard, and to be advanced 4 pence a yard for every 100 yards. (1798)
6. To make a Water level in the Hive Pit. (1798)
7. To make a drift in the Hive Pit. (1803)
8. To make a sump in the east workings of the Success Pit. (1804)

These agreements had to be tendered for by the workmen working.as a team. If their price for the task was acceptable to the manager, the task or bargain was awarded to them.

All these agreements were legal and binding between workmen and management.

7 Glossary

Apoplexy	Brain haemorrhage or stroke.
Back Shift	Working through the day.
Band	Strip of stone or impurities which is part of a coal seam.
Bank	Ground level
Bell Pits	A very early system of coal mining. A shaft was sunk to the coal seam and was worked outwards from the shaft, until, owing to poor ventilation and roof conition, it had to be abandoned. The finished pit was in the shape of a bell. When one closed another opened and the process started all over again. Consequently the country-side is littered with these.
Brake	A horse-drawn carriage carrying 12 to 20 people, very popular in the nineteenth century for outings .
Buzzer	Steam operated whistle.
Cages	A steel box suspended on the end of a winding rope to carry men and tubs into the mine shaft. (Invented by Mr. T.Y. Hall in 1835.)
Caunch	Stone left when coal had been extracted.
Cavil	Coal hewer's place of work.
Chaldron	A waggon with wooden wheels carrying 53 cwts (2.6 tonnes).
Checkweigh Man	A man employed and paid by the workmen to look after their interests. Usually Secretary of the Miners Lodge.
Coal Extraction	With some seams running close together the great problem was roof control. So for safety reasons the miners would extract as much coal as was possible in the first instnce. Then, conditions permitting, they would attempt a second extraction. This would continue until only Ribs and Stooks remained.
Coal Shift	Production shift, or coal drawing.
Colliery	A mine with shaft to mine deep seams of coal.

County Agreement	An agreement made between Management and Unions throughout the County.
Datal	A fixed daily rate of pay.
Drift	Underground tunnel driven to connect different seams
Drift Mine	A tunnel driven into a hillside to mine shallowseams of coal.
Dividend Day	Depending on your purchases over the preceding three months at the Co-op your divdend wold be estimated. The total sales of the Branch would be calculated and a dividend of x number of shillings to the pound would be declared. Your individual purchases would be totalled up and you would receive the appropriate payment e.g. two shillings for every pound you spent. That was your dividend.
Embankment	Land built up to provide a level bed for a waggonway.
Fore Shift	Working through the night: First Shift.
Goaves	Spaces left after coal had been extracted.
Guides	Between surface and shaft bottom stretched tight. The cages would run up and down between the guides keeping the cage stable while in motion.
Hewing	Digging coal.
In Bye	Going fom the shaft to your place of work.
Inspector of Mines	A man employed by the Government to enforce the Coal Mines Act.
Mechanics	Maintenance men employed at surface
Minimum or Mini Wage	The lowest possible piece work rate of pay.
Outburst	An exposed seam of coal. On seeing the outburst the owners of the land would begin a drift mine, to follow the coal horizontally within the boundaries of their royalty or mining rights.
Piece Work	A pay rate based on output.
Ribs and Stooks	Small pillars of coal left to support the roof when most of the coal had been extracted.

Ride	Ascend to surface at end of shift.
Rip	Explosives in stick form.
Rolley Way	A permanent track of iron rails for 8 cwt (0.39 tonnes) or 10 cwt (0.49 tonnes) tubs of coal to travel on, in sets of 30.
Rolling the Rig	Rolling the wicket or pitch in readiness for the cricket game.
Seam	Layers of compressed combustible material found at varying depths beteen layers of 'seatearth' .
Shaft	A vertical tunnel used to reach and mine deep coal seams.
Shift Work	Maintenance work an a much lower wage scale than piece work.
Staiths	Riverside coal drops where coal was loaded into boats.
Standage or sump	A place where water is collected.
Stapple	Small vertical shaft
Stop the Pit	Go on strike.
Sweeps or Sweepstakes	A race entry fee, the winner to take all the money .
Tommy Shop	A shop owned by a Coal Owner, who paid his miners in vouchers or tokens which had to be redeemed for goods at his shop .
Tubs	A four wheeled box carrying 8 cwt (0.39 tonnes) to 10 cwt (0.49 tonnes) of coal.
Waggonway	An early form of railway built to transport waggons from coal mines to staiths.
Water Level	A series of tunnels used to drain the water out of the collieries on higher ground.
Wayleave	A rent paid to the landowner for allowing the coal to be transported over his land.
Wheelwright	Skilled man for repairs of the Chaldron waggons.